ACT NOW

ACT NOW

THE FIRST EDITION

The Basic Study of Prevention

BOBAN KOVACEVIC

Library of Congress Control Number: 2024922186
ISBN: Hardcover   979-8-3694-3259-4
                   Softcover   979-8-3694-3260-0
                   eBook   979-8-3694-3261-7

Print information available on the last page.

Rev. date: 10/18/2024

To order additional copies of this book, contact:
Xlibris
844-714-8691
www.Xlibris.com
Orders@Xlibris.com
862844

CONTENTS

CHAPTER I

Free Gift from God

Prevention Is Better Than Cure
(1 Corinthians 7:25–31)

What Scripture Says about Preventing Sin?
Romans 6:12–14

"Therefore do not let sin reign in your mortal body, that you should obey it in its lusts. And do not present your members as instruments of unrighteousness to sin, but present yourselves to God as being alive from the dead, and your members as instruments of righteousness to God

What Is Crime Prevention?

Crime prevention is defined as "the anticipation, the recognition, and the appraisal of a crime risk and the initiation of action to remove or reduce it."

Crime prevention has been one of the primary mandates of police organizations since the establishment of the first modern style police agency, the London Metropolitan Police, in 1829. Throughout much of the twentieth century, US police agencies relied on three core operational strategies for preventing and controlling crime: random preventive patrol, rapid response to calls-for-service from citizens, and retrospective investigation of criminal offenses

What are some examples of crime prevention programs?

Many municipalities focus on neighborhood watch programs, citizen police academies, and similar community-based programs:

- senior citizen police academies
- youth police academies
- Coffee with a Cop
- National Night Out
- prescription drug drop-off locations
- home and business security surveys
- vacation property checks

The first step in crime prevention is to realize that in order to prevent crime or becoming a crime victim, we must accept that crime prevention is a shared responsibility. It is not a college problem or a police problem. It is a societal problem that can only be properly addressed by the entire campus community. On a college campus that includes students, faculty, staff, visitors, and neighbors. Therefore, campus safety is truly a shared responsibility.

Preventing Hate Crimes in Your Community

What is preventive action?

- Implementing safety training programs for employees.
- Performing regular maintenance operations on tools and equipment.
- Creating emergency plans in case of unexpected events, such as fires or natural disasters.
- Implementing an employee code of conduct.

CHAPTER II
Understand the Problem

Before a community addresses hate and bias-motivated crimes, all stakeholders need to understand the local problem. The best assessment method is the SARA model: scanning for the problems, analyzing the facts, responding to reduce the problems, and assessing the outcome of the response. The SARA model is primarily used by law enforcement to gain awareness and a better understanding of a problem. It can be applied to any situation and used by any group to address the unique issues facing the community.

The idea of preventing crime is a guiding principle of limited utility since each crime has its particular causes, patterns, victims, and consequences, and ways in which policing prevents crime is a function of the organization of policing.

Abstract

Policing is viewed quite broadly, particularly in relation to diverse ways that public and private protection and security function in contemporary societies, and policing varies in terms of organization, legal mandate, and territorial jurisdiction.

Further, substantial organizational specialization occurs within regional and large police departments, and specialized units vary in the scope of crime prevention activities. A common sense view of crime is that a visible police presence prevents people from committing crimes, either individually or in groups. Empirical studies, however, do not provide sufficient information on the role of police visibility in crime prevention. Somewhat paradoxically, both covert and visible policing can be used to prevent victimization by certain crime types. Surveillance is integral to protecting public and private interests, and most agencies with legal mandates to develop surveillance systems do so primarily to detect perpetrators as they are about to commit or actually commit a crime. The legitimate use of authority and coercion is a crime prevention technique, and dispute settlement is a primary concern of police since disputes can escalate into violent crimes. Other facets of crime prevention are examined, including access control, intelligence collection and analysis, research and development, police participation in community crime prevention programs and multiagency crime prevention efforts, problem-solving, and community policing.

Personal Security Tips

The following simple tips, when put into practice, can reduce the opportunity for you becoming a crime victim.

Criminals are constantly surveying the environment for an opportunity to commit crimes. Thieves will look for a running vehicle or an individual who leaves their valuables in the backseat of their vehicle.

Criminal opportunity is accomplished by a lack of witnesses or the creation of an easy target. The probability of being detected influences a criminal's decision to commit a crime. Increasing witness potential is one way to reduce criminal opportunity, but being more observant and aware of surroundings is another proactive method of enhancing your security. Don't make it easy for the criminal to make you a victim!

Methods of Reducing Criminal Opportunity

- Be alert and aware! While you are walking, keep your mind on what is going on around you. Knowing who is near is the first step to being secure. If someone makes you feel uncomfortable, move in the direction of other people.
- Display confidence. Walk with purpose, scan the area around you and make casual eye contact with others to display confidence. This reduces your chances of being targeted by criminals. Don't wear shoes or clothing that restrict your movements.
- Keep your hands free. Carrying items makes you a more vulnerable target for criminals. Backpacks should be worn on your back, keeping your arms and hands free. Avoid text messaging or lengthy cell phone use while walking alone. Be extra alert; know who and what are around you at all times.
- Trust your instincts. If you have an intuitive feeling something is wrong, trust your instincts. React immediately and take action to reduce your risk. Many individuals suppress these feelings because they fear their response will offend someone. React to your instincts and don't worry about someone else's feelings. If someone approaches you and you feel uncomfortable, move or ask for assistance. Call the police immediately

about all suspicious activity. Don't worry about bothering us because this is what we are here for.

- Ask for help. If you feel vulnerable, ask police or security to escort you to your car.

Theft Protection

- When leaving your dorm room, home, or office, lock doors and windows even if you will be gone for just a minute.
- Never leave your purse, wallet, or valuables exposed; store them out of sight. Be especially careful with your credit cards, which are very popular items among thieves because they are usually easy to steal and then use again. Consider obtaining a credit card with your photo imprinted on it.
- Computers, especially if they are portable, are primary targets of theft. Consider the purchase of a locking security or tracking device.
- Contact Public Safety to borrow engravers; engrave computers, stereos, and televisions with your driver's license number (including home state) or department name. Do not engrave on removable serial number plates.

Computer Scams

- Computer phishing is a crime. Phishers attempt to fraudulently acquire credit card details and other sensitive personal data via bogus email or pop-up windows. It may look like a legitimate email from a legitimate institution, but beware of unsolicited requests for information.

- Financial or payment institutions will never request that you send them personal sensitive data via email or pop-up windows.
- If you receive a suspicious looking email from any bank, lending, or payment institution, it is best to delete and not respond. If, by coincidence, you have an account with the entity mentioned in the email, call your legitimate institution using the number on your physical bill or via the telephone book or through telephone information.
- Do not call the number that may be listed in the bogus email and do not click on any link listed in the bogus email

Protecting Yourself from Identity Theft

- Destroy private records and statements. Destroy credit card statements, solicitations, and other documents that contain any private information. Shred this paperwork using a cross-cut shredder so thieves can't find your data when they rummage through your garbage. Also, don't leave a paper trail; never leave ATM, credit card, or gas station receipts behind.
- Secure your mail. Empty your mailbox quickly, lock it, or get a PO Box so criminals don't have a chance to steal credit card offers. Never mail outgoing bill payments and checks from an unsecured mailbox, especially at home. They can be stolen from your mailbox and the payee's name erased with solvents. Mail them from the post office or another secure location.
- Safeguard your Social Security number. Never carry your card with you or any other card that may have your number, like a health insurance card or school issued ID.

Don't put your number on your checks; your SSN is the primary target for identity thieves because it gives them access to your credit report and bank accounts. There are very few entities that can actually demand your SSN— the Department of Motor Vehicles, for example. Also, SSNs are required for transactions involving taxes, so that means banks, brokerages, employers, and the like also have a legitimate need for your SSN.

Automatic Teller Machines

- Try to use ATMs during daylight hours. If you must go at night, do not go alone.
- Avoid ATMs that are not well lit or clearly visible from the street.
- Be aware of people loitering or sitting in cars around ATMs.
- Prepare your transaction ahead of time. Do not spend much time at the machine.
- Do not give out your personal identification number (PIN) to anyone! Many thieves will attempt to steal your PIN number by calling you on the phone and claiming they are the police, security officers, or bank officers. Memorize it and do not keep a written copy of it in your wallet.
- Either keep your ATM receipt or tear it up and throw it away.

Vehicle Theft

- Always lock your car. Close windows all the way and make sure the trunk is locked.

- Even if you're rushed, look around before you get out and stay alert to the surroundings.
- Control your keys. Never leave an identification tag on your key ring. If your keys are lost or stolen, this could help a thief locate your car and burglarize your home.
- Keep everything of value you can in the trunk of your car. If you do leave packages, clothing, or other articles in the car, make sure they are out of sight or covered.
- Consider antitheft options, such as steering column locks, alarms, switches that interrupt fuel or electronic systems. Many insurance companies offer reduced rates to owners who install security devices.
- Keep your car's VIN (vehicle identification number), license plate number, and complete description in a safe place at home.

Social Media and Prevention

- When sharing pictures of your delicious meal on Instagram, tweeting about the horrific traffic, posting your resume on LinkedIn, and sharing on Facebook that you are checking into the resort with your friends for Senior Week, remember that information is out there for everyone to see. Although privacy settings and firewalls can protect you, the best way to stay safe when using social media is to be self-monitoring.
- Don't give out your personal information. Social media sites are a great way for you to express yourself and share the things you like with your friends. Be careful what you share. Don't post any of your personal information, such as your phone number, email address, birthday, or

home address. Make sure that you set strong privacy settings.

- Think about what you post. Don't post inappropriate comments, use foul language, or upload a picture that could get you in trouble. Everything that you post on a social media site has the potential of being copied and stored and can come back to haunt you. Potential employers may look at your social media site and deny you a position because of offensive posts and pictures.

- Send or accept friend requests only from people you know. An easy way to stay safe when using a social media site such as Facebook is to know who can see your profile. Make sure all of your friends are people you truly know.

- Be careful what you and your friends share. Ask your friends not to post pictures or videos you may be in or share conversations that you've had with them unless they have your permission. Privacy setting are available that require you to approve any post or comment before it attaches to your profile. And be sure to cover or turn off your laptop camera.

- Don't share your password with your friends. Aside from you and your parents, your password information is just that—yours. So don't share it with your friends. Your friends may want to play a harmless joke, but if they post something inappropriate under your name, it could get you in trouble.

- Control GPS-tracking settings. If you have a smartphone and you're using it to go on a social media site, see if you have enabled the geo-location service, and if so, turn it off. Facebook and Foursquare offer the feature to check in at registered locations. For example, if you're at the movies with a friend, you can tag both of you in at the theater and post it to your timeline. Using this feature lets everyone in your networks and those of your friends' networks know where you are, even those you may not want to know, and it also alerts wrongdoers to the fact that you are not home.

- Share your vacation plans and photos after you get home. Posting pictures and sharing your location lets everyone with access to your account know where you are. Don't advertise that your home is going to be empty.

CHAPTER III

Traffic and Safety Considerations for Travelers

More people are driving cars and riding motorcycles in destinations around the world. Accidents can happen anywhere; however, in some destinations, accidents are more likely as there may be poor road surfaces, roads without shoulders, unprotected curves and cliffs, or no streetlights. Also, traffic laws and road signs may not be regularly followed.

A crash or accident in another country may be more dangerous or likely to be fatal if emergency care is not be readily available. Consider the following questions before driving in another country:

- Are you comfortable driving in a new place?
- Do you know the local traffic rules and laws?
- Depending on your destination, are you comfortable driving on the left side of the road?

Traffic and Road Safety

Motor vehicle crashes are a leading cause of death among travelers. Follow these tips to reduce your risk of getting in an accident:

- Always wear a seat belt.
- If traveling with children, make sure you use appropriate car and booster seats. You may need to bring your own.
- Do not drive at night, especially in unfamiliar or rural areas.
- Do not ride motorcycles. If you must ride a motorcycle, wear a helmet.
- Know local traffic laws before you get behind the wheel.
- Do not drink and drive.
- Only ride in marked taxis, always wear a seatbelt when it is available.
- Avoid overcrowded, overweight, or top-heavy buses or vans.
- Do not use cell phones while driving

On Foot

- Avoid dark, vacant, or deserted areas; use well-lit routes.
- Avoid walking/jogging/running alone, especially at night. Ask a friend to go with you. Call Public Safety to accompany you around campus during evening hours.
- Dress in clothes and shoes that will not hamper movement.
- Be alert and aware of your surroundings at all times. Avoid wearing headsets that impair your ability to detect and respond to potentially dangerous situations.
- Report suspicious activity or noises immediately.

- Carry a noise-making device with you at all times, and use it if you suspect you are in danger. Move to a lit area or building and raise a commotion. Call 911 or activate a blue light emergency phone in the event of an emergency.

Bicycle Safety and Protection

- Use a bike light when riding a bicycle at night.
- Wear a helmet at all times when riding a bicycle.
- Obey all traffic laws; you must stop at intersections; pedestrians have the right of way.
- Pay attention to your surroundings; warn pedestrians when you are passing them.
- Take extra care when passing parking lot exits or driving through parking lots.
- Give proper hand signals when turning or stopping.
- Before leaving a lane, give a hand signal. Leave the lane only when safe to do so.
- Secure your bicycle with a heavy duty U-lock or chain. When possible, lock at least your front wheel and frame to a bike rack or other stationary object.
- Do not park your bicycle in a doorway, on stairs, or blocking any handicapped access. Use a bike rack.
- Engrave or permanently mark your bicycle with an identifying number and record that number with.

Improving Public Safety through Better Accountability and Prevention

Improving public safety requires a comprehensive set of accountability and prevention strategies that seek to change behavior while addressing the conditions giving rise to crime.

The officer assigned to serve as Crime Prevention Officer has been recognized as having strong skills in interpersonal relationships, planning and organization, research and analysis, writing and composition, as well as being comfortable in public speaking. Based on his or her proven work ethic, the crime prevention officer carries out the duties of the assignment with minimum direct supervision.

Duties of the Crime Prevention Officer include tasks, such as . . .

- Research and compilation of multiple inter-department monthly reports.
- Research and compose law enforcement and safety articles for publication and distribution to the community.
- Work cooperatively with concerned citizens to conduct crime prevention programs, community meetings and crime prevention training.
- Work with concerned neighborhoods to establish neighborhood watch programs Department at community meetings, Homeowners Association meetings, community sponsored safety events, and professional organizations.
- Serve as a social media administrator to manage the Police Department's website and social media. The Police Department's social media includes Facebook which provides weekly significant activity, safety tips, and event information.

Pedestrian Safety

- Pay attention when walking along or across roads, especially in countries where people drive on the left. Cross streets at a designated crosswalk or intersection whenever possible.

- Walk on a sidewalk or path instead of the road. If a path or sidewalk in not available, walk on the shoulder or side that lets you face oncoming traffic so you are more likely to see a dangerous situation and react before an accident occurs
- At night, carry a flashlight and wear reflective clothing. Avoid using electronic devices or wearing earbuds when walking. Do not go out walking if you have been drinking alcohol.

Protect Yourself When Driving

If you are driving near a disturbance, you should never drive through a crowd.

Here is how to stay safe:

- If you find yourself in the path of a crowd, turn down the nearest side road, turn around, and drive away calmly.
- If you cannot drive away, park the car, lock it, and leave it. Move to a safe area such as in a side street or doorway.
- If you don't have time for this, stop and turn the engine off. Lock the doors and remain calm. Be sure not to show hostility or anger.

Motor Vehicle Safety

- Park in well-lighted areas, where your vehicle is visible; avoid parking next to vans or trucks.
- Keep all items out of sight, especially valuables.
- Service your vehicle regularly to avoid breakdowns.
- Keep your vehicle locked at all times.

- When leaving your car for service, remove your other keys.
- Have your key ready when you approach your car. Before getting in, check inside and under your car to make sure no one is hiding.

CHAPTER IV

Crime Prevention Work in Community

It involves neighbors getting to know each other and working together in a program of mutual assistance; residents trained to recognize and report suspicious activities in their neighborhoods; and implementation of crime prevention techniques, such as home security, Operation Identification, etc.

Help to Organize a Community Violence Prevention Forum

Parents, school officials, and community members working together can be the most effective way to prevent violence in our schools.

Help Develop a School Violence Prevention and Response Plan

School communities that have violence prevention plans and crisis management teams in place are more prepared to identify and avert potential problems and to know what to do when a crisis happens.

Some Things You Can Do to Prevent Violence in Your School Community

Talk to Your Children

Keeping the lines of communication open with your children and teens is an important step to keeping involved in their schoolwork, friends, and activities.

Ask open-ended questions and use phrases such as "Tell me more" and "What do you think?" Phrases like these show your children that you are listening and that you want to hear more about their opinions, ideas, and how they view the world.

Start important discussions with your children—about violence, smoking, drugs, sex, drinking, death—even if the topics are difficult or embarrassing (read more about substance abuse). Don't wait for your children or teens to come to you. View our tips for discussing difficult situations with your child.

CHAPTER V

Prevention at Home

1.   Create a Fire Escape Plan

Does everyone in your house know what to do if a fire breaks out? If not, consider creating a fire escape plan that spells out critical details, such as how each person should exit the property and where the family should meet outside.

If you have children in your home, consider reviewing your fire escape plan at least once per year. You can even conduct an annual family fire drill to test everyone's knowledge of the plan.

2.   Install (and Maintain) Smoke Alarms

Smoke alarms can alert you if there's a fire before the situation gets out of control. Therefore, each level of your home should have at least one smoke alarm located in prime locations, such as the kitchen and bedrooms.

Because smoke alarms can only do their job when they're in working order, set a calendar reminder to change the batteries at least every year and replace the units every ten years. It's also recommended to test the alarms periodically to ensure they still work.

3. Have a Fire Extinguisher Handy (and Know How to Use It)

Quick thinking and action could save the day if a fire breaks out. In addition to knowing where the fire extinguisher is located in your home, everyone should be familiar with how to use it safely.

Depending on the size of your residence, it might make sense to have multiple units to cover the garage, kitchen, or other areas.

4. Understand Fire Safety Basics and Keep Your Home Safe

More than half of deaths from residential house fires occur between 11:00 p.m. and 7:00 a.m.—when most people are tucked away in bed. This means you'll want to take precautions to ensure your main living areas and bedrooms are as safe as possible.

Here are several ways to protect yourself and loved ones from fire hazards:

- Close your bedroom doors at night (this can slow down how quickly a blaze spreads).
- Use flame-retardant mattress covers.
- Ensure all candles, cigarettes, and incense burners are fully extinguished before going to sleep.
- Properly extinguish a fire and any ashes in a wood-burning fireplace; live ashes can take up to twenty-four hours to cool down

- Extinguish a grease fire quickly by covering it and depriving it of oxygen or use a nearby fire extinguisher

Carbon Monoxide Safety

Carbon monoxide is a colorless, odorless, and tasteless gas. As a result, victims of carbon monoxide poisoning are often unaware there's an issue. The good news is you can protect yourself and your family by taking a few critical steps:

1.   Install (and Maintain) Carbon Monoxide Detectors

Early detection is key to avoiding carbon monoxide poisoning. Having a detector on every level of your home can ensure you're notified if this gas is present. Be sure to replace the batteries every six months and install new units every five to seven years. You may also want to test each detector periodically to ensure they still work.

2.   Understand the Symptoms

Knowing the symptoms of carbon monoxide poisoning can help you escape a dangerous situation before it's too late. Some common signs include headache, nausea, vomiting, fatigue, lack of coordination, shortness of breath, dizziness, or mental confusion. If you or loved ones begin to feel these signs without other explanation, then get outside quickly and contact emergency medical services.

3.   Use and Maintain Equipment Properly

Charcoal, oil, and gasoline-burning equipment, such as generators, charcoal grills, camp stoves, or similar items, emit carbon monoxide. When using these devices, it's critical to have proper ventilation and never use them inside your home (including your basement or garage) or near a window. Also, avoid running your car inside your attached garage even if the garage door is open.

Broken or improperly maintained gas, oil, or coal-burning appliances and heating systems can also leak carbon monoxide into your home. Fortunately, you can significantly reduce that risk by having those units serviced annually by qualified technicians

Secure Doors and Windows

Even if you're just popping out for a quick errand, remember to lock your doors and windows. It's a simple yet effective deterrent for potential intruders.

Valuables Placement

Keep valuable items out of sight from prying eyes outside your home. Don't make it easy for opportunistic thieves.

Lighting

As the days grow shorter, consider using timers to light up your home's interior and exterior. This gives the illusion that someone is home, making your property less appealing to criminals.

Landscaping

Maintain clear visibility around your home by keeping vegetation in check. Tall trees and shrubs should not obstruct windows, and consider planting thorny plants near vulnerable entry points.

Cardboard Disposal

Dispose of cardboard boxes properly to avoid broadcasting your recent purchases to potential thieves.

Security Alarm: Invest in a Monitor

Take Vacations Quietly

Next time you decide to take a trip, don't make it obvious. Burglars love to target empty houses because there's less risk of confrontation. You can make it seem like you're still home by putting your lights on an automatic timer, having someone park in your driveway, and asking your neighbor to collect your mail. In addition, avoid talking about your getaway on social media (especially on public profiles) until after you return.

Protect Your Home the Better Way

The best way to safeguard your home and family from risk is to be proactive and implement crucial safety measures like the ones outlined above. But a comprehensive homeowner's insurance policy can take your protection to the next level.

Some homeowner's insurance, like some provided through Better Cover, even offer discounts on your policy for installing an alarm system. And if you use your Better Home Card to finance the installation, you'll benefit from a competitive interest rate and will have three.

CHAPTER VI

Workplace Injury Prevention Tips for Ten Common Injuries

Home, workplace, illness, and injury workplace injury prevention tips for ten common injuries

As a business owner, you've spent years building a staff that does their work well and coordinates as a team. Anything that threatens that balance—such as a workers comp claim—should be avoided.

Workplace accidents and injuries not only affect your insurance premiums, they can also have a devastating impact on productivity. Workplace injury prevention is just good business practice.

Here are the ten most common workplace injury examples, plus some steps you can take—as an employee or a supervisor—to avoid tragedy and maintain a safe work environment.

1. Slips, Trips, and Falls

According to the National Safety Council, slip-and-fall accidents are responsible for 25 percent of all work-related injuries, regardless of industry.

Slips, trips, and falls are some of the most common workplace injuries because they can occur in so many different ways. A puddle on the floor of a restaurant kitchen, an unstable ladder, an unsecured rug—any of these safety hazards have the potential to disrupt an orderly workplace.

Work Boot about to Step on Banana Peel

This is a shame because slip and fall accidents are relatively easy to prevent. Here are some steps you can take to prevent fall-related injuries at work.

- Keep floors clear of clutter, debris, and spills.
- Make sure work areas are well lit.
- Maintain the work environment and repair hazardous areas.
- Install signs that warn employees of potential workplace hazards.
- Wear proper shoes.
- Add nonskid floor coverings in high-risk areas.
- Make sure there are adequate handrails on stairways.
- Perform a slip and fall audit of the work environment to identify any hazards. This will help you create an easy-to-follow to-do list for good workplace injury prevention.

Injured at work in Florida?

Let's talk.

2. Cuts and Lacerations

It's not only machinists and restaurant workers that need to worry about getting cut on the job. Retail employees are especially vulnerable to cuts and lacerations at work, as they are typically under a time-sensitive deadline (especially for seasonal employment during the holiday season) and rarely receive formal training on how to handle a box cutter safely.

The majority of workplace cuts and lacerations can be prevented by properly training employees on how to work with knives, box cutters, scissors, and other sharp objects.

- Keep cutting edges sharp; dull knives require more force, which can cause the blade to slip.
- Store cutting implements safely when not in use.
- Wear properly fitting protective gloves.
- Remind employees not to rush.
- Train employees to pull box cutters toward them (instead of pushing away) to open boxes.

When it comes to cuts and lacerations, the main responsibility of injury prevention lies with your employees. Reminding them of proper workplace safety will reduce accidents and injuries, claims, and time off from work.

3. Muscle Strain

Muscle strain is a very common injury in the manufacturing industry, but any job position runs the risk of pulling your back out. Even moving a box of copy paper out of the supply room can cause a serious injury.

In fact, it's typically workers in these more "office-related" environments that are more prone to injury; workplace safety training isn't typically part of employee on-boarding.

Man Bending over to Lift Cardboard Box

- Encourage employees to stretch or do warm-up exercises before shifting heavy objects. Warming muscles and tendons decreases the risk of strains and sprains.
- Provide ergonomic equipment to make lifting and moving heavy objects easier.
- Provide mechanical assistance when needed (i.e., forklifts, carts, etc.)
- Train employees on proper lifting technique.
- Set a 51-lb. per person weight limit on lifting objects.

4. Machine Entanglement

It's both unfortunate and counterintuitive that the more experience someone has working on a machine, the more prone they are to injuring themselves on it. More experienced employees tend to exercise less caution and, naturally, lack of caution increases the likelihood of an injury.

Becoming entangled in heavy machinery can lead to amputation and even death (far more serious injuries than a slip on a wet floor).

Make sure all machine workers follow these safety guidelines at all times:

- Avoid wearing loose clothing and/or jewelry. Long sleeves, necklaces, and other items can be easily grabbed by a machine's parts.
- Wear long hair up in a bun. Loose hair, even ponytails, can easily become entangled in a machine.
- Steer clear of heavy machines while they are in operation. Do not try to climb over, under, or around them until they have been shut off.
- Make sure all stop-time measurements are accurate and remind employees to wait the proper length of time after the machine is turned off before attempting to work on it.
- Encourage employees to stretch or do warm-up exercises before shifting heavy objects. Warming muscles and tendons decreases the risk of strains and sprains.
- Provide ergonomic equipment to make lifting and moving heavy objects easier.
- Provide mechanical assistance when needed (i.e. forklifts, carts,

Here are some steps you can take to prevent fall-related injuries at work.

- Keep floors clear of clutter, debris, and spills.
- Make sure work areas are well lit.
- Maintain the work environment and repair hazardous areas.
- Install signs that warn employees of potential workplace hazards.
- Wear proper shoes.

CHAPTER VII

Religion and Prevention

This study reviews the voluminous empirical evidence on faith's contribution to preventing people from falling victim to substance abuse and helping them recover from it. We find that 73 percent of addiction treatment programs in the USA include a spirituality-based element, as embodied in the twelve-step programs and fellowships initially popularized by Alcoholics Anonymous—the vast majority of which emphasize reliance on God or a Higher Power to stay sober. We introduce and flesh out a typology of faith-based substance abuse treatment facilities, recovery programs, and support groups. This typology provides important background as we then move on to make an economic valuation of nearly 130,000 congregation-based substance abuse recovery support programs in the USA. We find that these faith-based volunteer support groups contribute up to $316.6 billion in savings to the US economy every year at no cost to tax payers. While negative experiences with religion (e.g., clergy sex abuse and other horrendous examples) have been a contributory factor to substance abuse among some victims, given that more than 84 percent of scientific studies show that faith is a positive factor in addiction prevention or recovery and a risk in less than 2 percent of the studies reviewed, we conclude that the value of faith-oriented approaches to substance abuse prevention and recovery is indisputable. And, by extension, we also conclude that the decline in religious affiliation in the USA is not only a concern for religious organizations but constitutes a national health concern.

Islam places a strong emphasis on prevention in its teachings on health, safety, and disease prevention. The concept of prevention, *wiqayat*, is considered a fixed law of Allah and involves using limited human knowledge to anticipate disease conditions and take preventative measures.

Buddhism encourages its people to avoid self-indulgence but also self-denial. Buddha's most important teachings, known as the Four Noble Truths, are essential to understanding the religion. Buddhists embrace the concepts of karma (the law of cause and effect) and reincarnation (the continuous cycle of rebirth).

Buddhism has a philosophy of "prevention before disease" that is based on the practice of meditation and mindfulness.

Jewish World and Prevention

Instead, the path to peace and unity is to make unity bigger and more fundamental than the principle or perspective you might have. We are brothers first and foremost. Before we even open our mouths to share our opinions. And if we do need to disagree, it's with an arm around the other person in friendship, exuding care, understanding, empathy and love, rather than animosity, disdain, invalidation and contempt.

"We must expand our investment in preventing violent conflict and mass atrocities from breaking out, and also seek to find solutions to ongoing conflicts, to mitigate further loss of life and additional displacement. A durable peace, one that addresses and seeks to resolve the root causes and drivers of the conflict, must be sought for ongoing conflicts. This is the only way to break the cycle of violence. Short-term and weak peace agreements continue to fail and often cause further conflict.

"We need long-term solutions to these problems, and we need strong leadership to help us achieve those solutions."

CHAPTER VIII

Talking Openly about the Blight of Suicide

We face a global mental health epidemic. When people are suffering from untreated, severe mental illnesses and emotional disorders, suicide becomes a real and present danger. According to a World Health Organization (WHO) report published in 2014, 800,000 individuals worldwide were committing suicide each year, meaning one person every forty seconds. Statistically, teenagers, university students, and young adults died of suicide most often. Men were overwhelmingly more likely to die in violent suicides. An increase in mental health problems preceded COVID-19, but the pandemic has heightened mental stresses, with a correlating rise of suicides, especially among young people in the US.

Suicide is commonly divided into two categories. First, there are individuals who plan, organize, and write suicide notes in advance of their death. Second are those who turn to suicide because they feel unable to control their emotions when overwhelmed. Psychologists and sociologists have different theories about why people kill themselves. There may be external causes that lead to great physical suffering, such as severe injury or extreme poverty. Such suffering often extends to emotional trauma, grief, or turmoil, although the emotional factor can often be its own cause for suicide. Frequently, there are subjective and extremely intense feelings of insult, shame, failure, or humiliation, which the individual is unable to endure, leading to the conclusion that death is unequivocally better than living with intense social stigma or personal shame.

In the latter case of social shame, we can see how young people might turn to suicide as a result of perceived failure. The perceived failure—perhaps the inability to pass an exam, the loss of a job opportunity, or a romantic breakup—can lead to a sense of disgrace, humiliation, or shame. Such feelings can be due to personal expectations, but they are often imposed from without by the culture, family life, and societal values in which young people find themselves. Emotions can therefore be volatile upon suffering these perceived failures. Parental pressure can be overwhelming when children fail to attain desired or expected exam results. Young people may find themselves socially ostracized after a breakup or suffer romantic rejection. Or, as is particularly common in the post-COVID era, they might feel a deepening sense of loneliness that social media cannot resolve, with a lack of meaningful social bonds that would offset any sense of stalled progress or regression

Helping a loved one deal with depression can be the key to their recovery. It isn't always going to be easy. But there are some things that can help:

Learn the facts. The first thing to do is discover as much as you can about depression. Read up on the causes and treatments and what you can do to help.

Get other people involved. You can't do this alone. Your friend or loved one may want you to keep their depression a secret. That isn't healthy. It puts far too much pressure on you.

Try to get a small circle of family and friends to pitch in. That way, you can help look after your loved one together.

Ask what they need. Be direct. Unless you ask, you won't know what your friend or loved one wants from you.

Don't try to solve the problem. To get better, your person needs professional help from a doctor or therapist. Depression is a medical illness. You wouldn't try to cure a friend's diabetes on your own. You shouldn't try curing depression, either.

Encourage your friend or loved one to stick with their treatment plan and to eat well, get enough sleep, and stay away from alcohol and drugs.

Offer to help with the practical things. If you have depression, it's easy to feel overwhelmed. Everyday stuff—dressing the kids for school, grocery shopping, or laundry—can feel like too much. Pitch in. Sometimes, a little help with the day-to-day things can make a big difference.

Invite your friend or loved one to be active and social. Depressed people tend to isolate themselves, which can make things worse. But don't push too hard. If they already feel overwhelmed, they may pull back even more

Is My Friend an Alcoholic?

There are many different signs for how to tell if your friend's drinking has crossed into the realm of alcohol misuse. Having an occasional drink is not a problem, but if your friend is drinking heavily or seems to be unable to control how much they drink, these are symptoms of alcohol misuse or alcoholism. If your friend becomes violent when drinking, drives while drunk, or drinks at inappropriate times, these behaviors may also indicate a problem

How to Talk to a Friend about Their Drinking

It's probably not going to be easy to have the conversation, but preparing yourself in advance can help. Writing down your concerns in a list can help you organize your thoughts and feelings. It can also be useful to refer to your list during the conversation to help you stay on track. It's also a good idea to wait until your friend isn't under the influence. Otherwise, they will probably be less willing to hear your concerns. Choose a quiet moment in a private setting with few distractions, such as at home or on a walk.

Have you ever thought to yourself "My friend drinks too much" or "Is my friend an alcoholic"? If you are worried about them and are wondering how to help, you first need to determine whether your friend truly needs help and whether or not they are ready to accept help. Educating yourself is another step on the path to knowing how to deal with an alcoholic friend and be able to give them the support they need. Once your friend decides to seek help for their addiction, you should be ready to offer help and make recommendations about treatment programs.

Remember, it's your choice.

How you think about any decision to change can affect your success. Many people who decide to cut back or quit drinking think, "I am not allowed to drink," as if an external authority were imposing rules on them. Thoughts like this can breed resentment and make it easier to give in. It's important to challenge this kind of thinking by telling yourself that you are in charge, that you know how you want your life to be, and that you have decided to make a change.

Similarly, you may worry about how others will react or view you if you make a change. Again, challenge these thoughts by remembering that it's your life and your choice, and that your decision should be respected.

Plan ahead to stay in control.

Even if you are committed to changing your drinking, social pressure to drink from friends or others can make it hard to cut back or quit. This short activity offers a recognize-avoid-cope approach commonly used in cognitive-behavioral therapy, which helps people to change unhelpful thinking patterns and reactions. It also provides links to worksheets to help you get started with your own plan to resist pressure to drink.

Recognize two types of pressure.

The first step is to become aware of the two different types of social pressure to drink alcohol—direct and indirect.

Direct social pressure is when someone offers you a drink or an opportunity to drink.

Indirect social pressure is when you feel tempted to drink just by being around others who are drinking—even if no one offers you a drink.

Take a moment to think about situations where you feel direct or indirect pressure to drink or to drink too much. You can use the form linked below to write them down. Then, for each situation, choose some resistance strategies from below, or come up with your own. When you're done, you can print the form.

Avoid pressure when possible.

For some situations, your best strategy may be avoiding them altogether. If you feel guilty about avoiding an event or turning down an invitation, remind yourself that you are not necessarily talking about forever. When you have confidence in your resistance skills, you may decide to ease gradually into situations you now choose to avoid. In the meantime, you can stay connected with friends by suggesting alternate activities that don't involve drinking.

Gambling Problem Prevention

About the Problem

Gambling becomes problem gambling when it negatively affects a person's life or the lives of their family, friends, or coworkers. Some populations have a higher risk for developing problem gambling, including youth, men, and people of color.

Gambling problem has a high comorbidity with substance misuse and mental health conditions; this means that a person often has all three conditions at the same time. Gambling problem is also associated with poor health and suicide.

Prevention Approaches

Prevention plays an important role in reducing the harmful effects of problem gambling. Some effective prevention practices include the following:

- Change the conditions in the environment
- Support the development of knowledge and skills

- Ensure prevention efforts are tailored to a population's level of risk
- Ensure prevention efforts are integrated into existing public health prevention efforts
- Problem gambling prevention approaches include the Photovoice Project, the Ambassador Project, and the Community Health Worker Pilot Project.

CHAPTER IX
Defensible Space

The defensible space theory was developed in the 1980s by architect Oscar Newman which postulated that architectural and environmental designs play a crucial part in increasing/reducing criminality in a neighborhood.

Defensible space is defined as "a residential environment whose physical characteristics allow its inhabitants to themselves become key agents in ensuring its security." An area is safer when its inhabitants feel a sense of ownership and responsibility toward it and a building's design can itself help its inhabitants to police the area around it.

In 1982, James Wilson and George Kelling first introduced the broken windows theory in an article in the *Atlantic Monthly* with this line, "If a window in a building is broken and left unrepaired, all the rest of the windows will soon be broken." One unrepaired broken window is a signal that no one cares, and so breaking more windows costs nothing.

Later, in 1996, Kelling along with Catharine Coles authored *Fixing Broken Windows* which discussed the theory in relation to crime and crime prevention in urban areas. They claimed that improving the quality of the neighborhood environment reduces petty crime, antisocial behavior, and low-level disorders, resultantly reducing major crimes

Containment and the Truman Policy

The Truman Doctrine, also known as the policy of containment, was President Harry Truman's foreign policy that the US would provide political, military, and economic aid to democratic countries under the threat of communist influences in order to prevent the expansion of communism.

The policy marked a step away from America's previous isolationist policies, which discouraged the US from becoming involved in foreign affairs.

CHAPTER X
Prevention in Old Egypt and Greece

The Pharaohs were advanced in many fields, especially in the field of medicine; in their era, they were not subjected to epidemics because they were keen on eating healthy foods.

According to a study titled "How the Ancient Egyptians Practiced Medicine," the ancient Egyptians believed that the disease was mostly due to the wrath of the gods or evil spirits and magic.

Also, they believed that pleasing the gods would lead to healing, and this is what they did with some of the gods, such as Sekhmet and the sun god Ra.

The electronic magazine *Al-Tibbi* published a report entitled "Ancient Egyptian Medicine" that indicated that the ancient Egyptians believed that physical health is linked to spiritual health, and in the event of illness, therapists are advised to pray.

The report, which was published through Listverse, stated that the Pharaohs used preventive drugs to maintain their health and strengthen their immune system and that they took special care of their diet.

They ate more onions, garlic, and foods rich in antioxidants and vitamin A. This reduced their chances of catching diseases.

If those of us involved in the world of infection control and prevention lived in Ancient Greece, we would have surely found a home in the followers of Hygieia, the mythical goddess of cleanliness and sanitation and the origin of the word hygiene. While her sisters were worrying about healing, recuperation, and remedy, Hygieia was working to prevent illness by cleaning and advocating sanitary practices. (Sound familiar?) In today's post, the last in our series recognizing Women's History Month, we'll take a look at this figure, what she represented, and what she can teach us about the origins of the field of infection prevention.

The ancient Greek pantheon have a well-established legacy in the Western world despite losing their religious following millennia ago. Not only do they survive as figures and inspiration in the arts and philosophy, many of their names persist in the language of sciences, including medicine. We have all read about breakthroughs in drug *therapies*—a word we get from the Greek term "therapeutae" for the caretakers of the temples of Asclepius, the god of medicine. You will surely recognize one such *therapeutai*: Hippocrates.

According to Greek mythology, the children of Asclepius were also engaged in the practices of healing and health. One of his daughters, Panacea, gives her name to a word we still use today to mean a "universal remedy." She, her father, and sister Hygieia were invoked during the earliest form of the Hippocratic Oath, which begins with the famous words "First, do no harm."

Hygieia became an important goddess to the ancient civilizations of Greece and Rome during the massive Plague of Athens (430–427 BC) and Rome (293 BC). Why the goddess of cleanliness and sanitation? During this time period, physicians had only just begun to operate under the Hippocratic theory that disease was caused by nature rather than by the gods. While they did not yet understand the germ theory of disease, they tried to use observation, record-keeping, and experimentation to solve health crises. This theory was far from perfect, but it had just enough grounding in what would become the scientific method that their observations shed some light on how to prevent disease. One of the most important realizations to emerge was the role of cleanliness and sanitation. No longer were individuals depending purely on praying to their gods to avoid sickness, they were also taking their own precautions to keep themselves healthy.